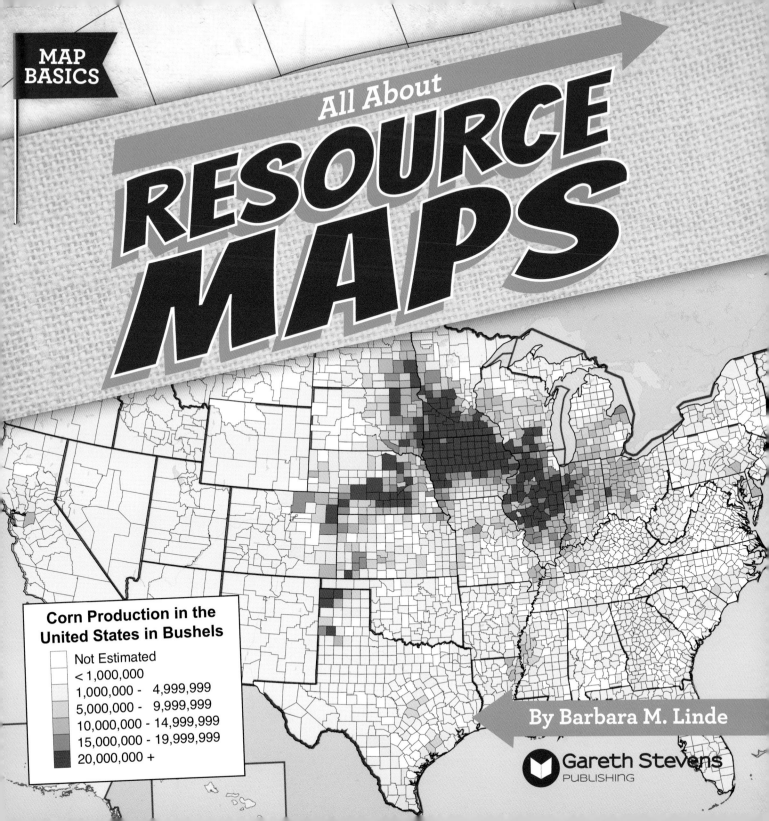

MAP
BASICS

All About

RESOURCE
MAPS

By Barbara M. Linde

Corn Production in the United States in Bushels

	Not Estimated
	< 1,000,000
	1,000,000 - 4,999,999
	5,000,000 - 9,999,999
	10,000,000 - 14,999,999
	15,000,000 - 19,999,999
	20,000,000 +

Gareth Stevens
PUBLISHING

Please visit our website, www.garethstevens.com. For a free color catalog of all our high-quality books, call toll free 1-800-542-2595 or fax 1-877-542-2596.

Cataloging-in-Publication Data
Names: Linde, Barbara M.
Title: All about resource maps / Barbara M. Linde.
Description: New York : Gareth Stevens Publishing, 2019. | Series: Map basics | Includes glossary and index.
Identifiers: ISBN 9781538232668 (pbk.) | ISBN 9781538229187 (library bound) | ISBN 9781538232675 (6pack)
Subjects: LCSH: Maps–Juvenile literature. | Natural resources–Juvenile literature. | Map reading–Juvenile literature.
Classification: LCC GA105.6 L56 2019 | DDC 912–dc23

Published in 2019 by
Gareth Stevens Publishing
111 East 14th Street, Suite 349
New York, NY 10003

Designer: Sarah Liddell
Editor: Monika Davies

Photo credits: Cover, pp. 1, 5 United States Department of Agriculture/Derfel73/Wikimedia Commons; p. 7 georgeclerk/E+/Getty Images; pp. 9, 11, 13, 17, 19 (map) ekler/Shutterstock.com; pp. 11, 15 (mining symbol) Victor Z/Shutterstock.com; p. 11 (peanut symbol) samoyloff/Shutterstock.com; pp. 11, 15 (cattle, corn, grains, hogs, poultry, sheep, manufacturing, oil and gas, and fishing symbols) CharacterFamily/Shutterstock.com; p. 13 (lettuce and rice) Hennadii H/Shutterstock.com; p. 13 (maple syrup) Anna.zabella/Shutterstock.com; p. 13 (peanut, beans, macadamia nut, and lentils) sasimoto/Shutterstock.com; p. 13 (apple, grape, chile pepper, orange, watermelon, cherry, cranberry, potato, sweet potato, beet, pumpkin, and tomato) Maxito/Shutterstock.com; p. 15 (map) pingebat/Shutterstock.com.

Printed in the United States of America

CPSIA compliance information: Batch #CW19GS: For further information contact Gareth Stevens, New York, New York at 1-800-542-2595.

CONTENTS

Words in the glossary appear in **bold** type the first time they are used in the text.

WHAT ARE RESOURCE MAPS?

Maps are drawings that give information about a city, state, or other place. Resource maps show where resources are produced or found naturally. By looking at a resource map, you can figure out which countries have gold mines. You can also see where cattle are raised.

People use resource maps for many reasons. A company that makes wooden furniture might want to build its factory near a forest. A farmer looking for a job might look at a resource map to find out where corn is grown.

JUST THE FACTS

You can compare resource maps with other types of maps to learn more about where resources are found and used.

UNITED STATES CORN PRODUCTION

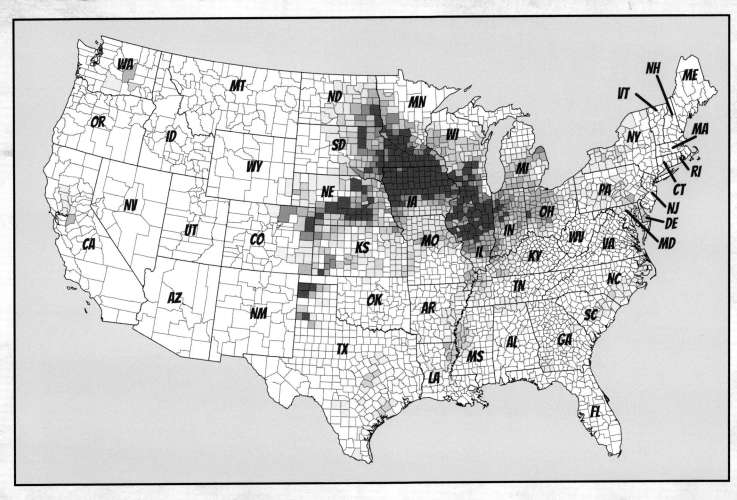

BUSHELS:

NOT ESTIMATED	UNDER 1,000,000	1,000,000–4,999,999	5,000,000–9,999,999	10,000,000–14,999,999	15,000,000–19,999,999	OVER 20,000,000

This resource map shows where the most **bushels** of corn were produced in the United States in 2010. Some maps show resource locations in this way. Others use **symbols**.

TYPES OF RESOURCES

A resource is something that can be used by people. Natural resources are one type of resource. A natural resource is something found in nature. If you eat fruits and vegetables, have furniture made from wood, or wear cotton clothes, you're using natural resources!

Agricultural products are another type of resource. They include crops, or plants that farmers grow. Common types of crops are corn, wheat, potatoes, and rice. Livestock, such as cattle, sheep, and chickens, are also agricultural products.

Lumber is wood that has been cut into logs or boards. It's a resource produced and used by people around the world.

7

MINING MINERALS

Resource maps often use symbols to stand for the different resources found in an area. The legend, or map key, explains what the symbols mean.

Minerals are natural resources found inside Earth. People mine, or dig out, minerals and use them to make items such as coins, jewelry, and computer parts. This map of Africa shows where different types of minerals are found. The legend has a symbol for each mineral. For example, you can see that diamonds are found in southern and western Africa.

JUST THE FACTS

Minerals are found in many objects you use every day, including light bulbs, batteries, computers, and mobile phones!

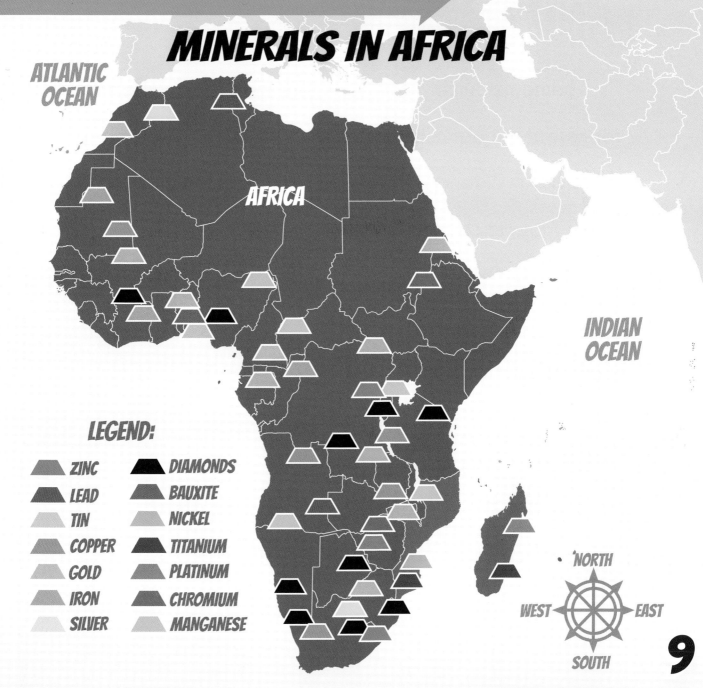

This resource map shows the many mineral resources in Africa. Besides diamond, there's nickel, zinc, copper, and more!

MINERALS IN AFRICA

ATLANTIC OCEAN

AFRICA

INDIAN OCEAN

LEGEND:

ZINC

LEAD

TIN

COPPER

GOLD

IRON

SILVER

DIAMONDS

BAUXITE

NICKEL

TITANIUM

PLATINUM

CHROMIUM

MANGANESE

NORTH

WEST

EAST

SOUTH

9

LAND USE

Some resource maps use more than just symbols to **represent** the agricultural products produced in an area. If large areas of land are used for the same purpose, these areas may be colored in the background.

For example, the medium green area on this map of Oklahoma shows that much of the state's land is used for growing crops. You can also see that forest areas are found to the east and livestock grazing areas are found mostly in the north.

LAND USE IN OKLAHOMA

KANSAS

TEXAS

OKLAHOMA

•TULSA

•OKLAHOMA CITY

0.75 INCH
—————
50 MILES

LEGEND:

▢ LIVESTOCK GRAZING	▢ CROPLAND	◼ URBAN AREA	▢ FOREST
🐂 CATTLE	🍎 FRUIT	🏭 MANUFACTURING	🌽 PEANUTS
🌽 CORN	🌾 GRAINS	⚒ MINING	🐓 POULTRY
🌿 COTTON	🐖 HOGS	🛢 OIL/GAS	🐑 SHEEP

It's clear from this map that much of the land in Oklahoma is used for agricultural purposes. Can you find the **urban** areas on the map? Use the scale to figure out how far apart they are.

NORTH

WEST — EAST

SOUTH

11

WHERE THE CROPS GROW

The compass rose shows directions. North is usually shown at the top of the map, and south is shown at the bottom. East is to the right, and west is to the left.

Crops are natural resources people use for food, to feed animals, or to make other products.

This map shows the top crop in each US state. Using the compass rose, you can see that many southern states grow peanuts, while apples grow well in the East.

JUST THE FACTS

Arkansas is the top rice-growing state with over 2,700 rice farms.

UNITED STATES CROPS

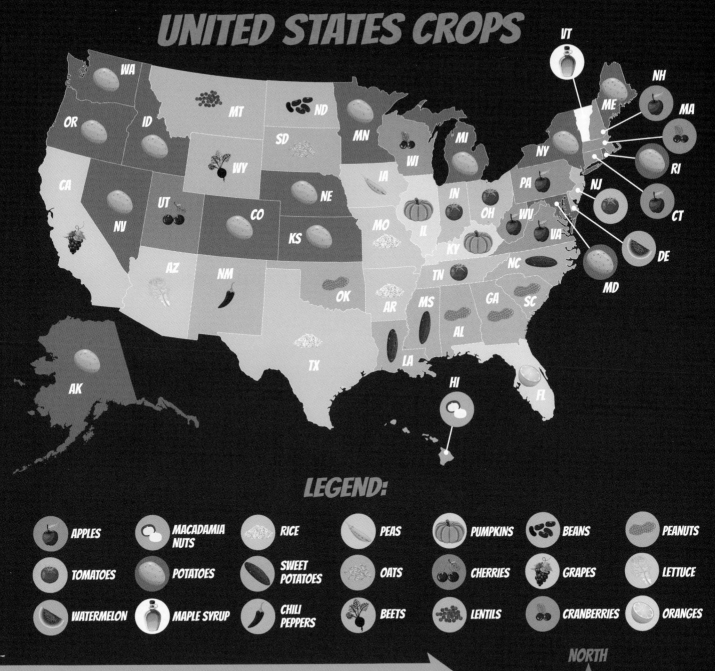

LEGEND:

- APPLES
- MACADAMIA NUTS
- RICE
- PEAS
- PUMPKINS
- BEANS
- PEANUTS
- TOMATOES
- POTATOES
- SWEET POTATOES
- OATS
- CHERRIES
- GRAPES
- LETTUCE
- WATERMELON
- MAPLE SYRUP
- CHILI PEPPERS
- BEETS
- LENTILS
- CRANBERRIES
- ORANGES

In 2016, two-thirds of the United States' fruits and nuts were grown in sunny California.

NORTH
WEST — EAST
SOUTH

RESOURCES AROUND THE WORLD

Resource maps can be used to compare where resources are found around the world. This can help businesses that want to use certain resources figure out where to buy or make goods. People can also use resource maps to see what kinds of jobs there might be in a certain country.

On this map, you can see that mineral mines are found in Canada. This means mining jobs are likely available there. Wheat is also grown in Canada, which means there's also a need for farmers.

JUST THE FACTS

Resource maps usually don't show exactly where a resource is located. They often just show the general area where you can find the resource.

RESOURCES IN CANADA

LEGEND:

CATTLE	FISHING	FORESTRY	FRUIT	HOGS	MINING	OIL/GAS	WHEAT/GRAINS

Alberta, a **province** in Canada, has a large supply of oil.

WIND POWER

Wind is a **renewable** natural resource because it's a resource that will never run out. This is because wind will always keep blowing. Wind farms use machines called turbines to turn wind power into electricity. Turbines have large, long blades. Wind turns these long blades in circles, which powers the turbines' **generators** to produce electrical energy.

Turbines are often located in places that are very windy, such as areas along coastlines. Resource maps can show you the places that use wind power to make electricity.

JUST THE FACTS
A nonrenewable resource is something that isn't replaceable by nature. It will run out one day. For example, coal is a nonrenewable resource that we also use for power.

This map shows where wind turbines are found in Italy. Use the compass rose to explain where the country's greatest number of wind turbines are located.

WIND TURBINES IN ITALY

NORTH

WEST   EAST

SOUTH

NUMBER OF TURBINES:

•	•	●	●	●	●
10	100	250	500	1,000	3,000

LIVESTOCK RESOURCES

Chickens are a type of livestock and a source of food for people all over the world. In the United States, broiler chickens are a type of young chicken produced on farms for food.

This resource map shows where broiler chickens are produced in the United States. The dark blue states are where the most broiler chickens are produced. For example, 651.2 million chickens were produced in Texas. Arkansas, Alabama, and Georgia each produced over 1 billion chickens!

JUST THE FACTS

In 2017, over 9 billion broiler chickens were produced in the United States.

BROILER CHICKEN PRODUCTION IN THE UNITED STATES

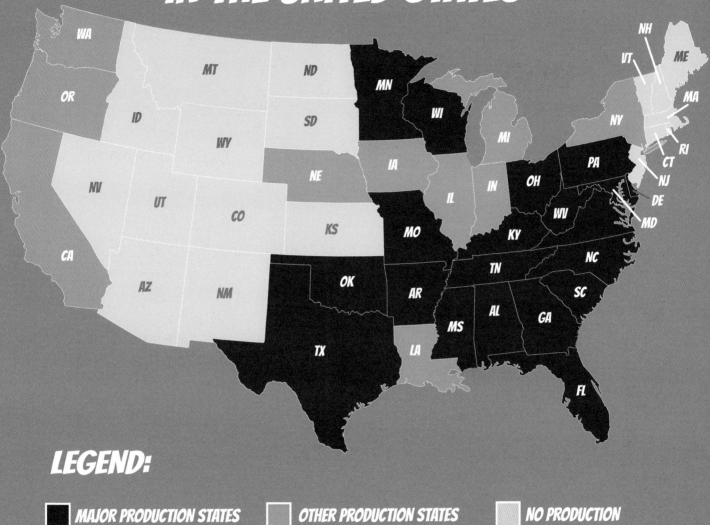

LEGEND:

■ MAJOR PRODUCTION STATES □ OTHER PRODUCTION STATES ▨ NO PRODUCTION

The states that are shaded dark blue produce 93.6 percent of broiler chickens in the United States. States colored in light blue raise the rest, and states shown in gray don't have broiler chicken farms.

MAP IT!

What resources are found and produced in your state? What do you know about the resources of other states?

Work with a partner or a small group. Choose a state and **research** its resources. Look up the state's most popular crops, minerals, and livestock. What other resources are found or made there? Also research how the state uses its land. Create a resource map and show it to your classmates. How do the resources in your state compare to those of your classmates' states?

MAKE YOUR OWN RESOURCE MAP!

1 CHOOSE A STATE. USE PRINT OR ONLINE SOURCES FOR YOUR RESEARCH. USE KEY WORDS SUCH AS *NATURAL RESOURCES, MINERALS, LIVESTOCK,* AND *CROPS.*

2 WRITE DOWN THE NAME OF EACH RESOURCE AND ITS LOCATION.

3 GET A LARGE SHEET OF PAPER AND COLORED MARKERS. PUT THE NAME OF THE STATE AT THE TOP OF THE PAPER. DRAW THE OUTLINE OF THE STATE. THEN, DRAW THE STATE'S BODIES OF WATER IN BLUE.

4 MAKE A LEGEND THAT HAS A SYMBOL FOR EACH OF THE STATE'S RESOURCES.

5 DRAW SYMBOLS ON THE MAP TO SHOW WHERE TO FIND EACH RESOURCE. REMEMBER TO INCLUDE A COMPASS ROSE. YOU CAN ALSO TRY MAKING A SCALE.

GLOSSARY

agricultural: having to do with farming

bushel: a unit of measurement. One bushel equals about 9 gallons (35 l).

distance: the amount of space between two places or things

economic: having to do with the economy, or the money made in an area and how it's made

generator: a machine that uses moving parts to produce electrical energy

province: an area of a country

renewable: able to be replaced by nature

represent: to stand for

research: studying to find something new

scale: a line on a map that shows a specific unit of measure (such as an inch) used to represent a larger unit (such as a mile)

symbol: a picture, shape, or object that stands for something else

urban: having to do with the city

FOR MORE INFORMATION

BOOKS

National Geographic Society. *National Geographic Kids United States Atlas*. Washington, DC: National Geographic, 2017.

Olien, Rebecca. *Map Keys*. New York, NY: Children's Press, 2013.

Overend Prior, Jennifer. *Our Natural Resources*. Huntington Beach, CA: Teacher Created Materials, 2015.

WEBSITES

Electricity Generation from Renewable Energy
www.nationalgeographic.org/maps/electricity-generation-renewable-energy-sources
Check out these maps to see which countries use renewable sources to create energy.

State Agricultural Facts
www.agclassroom.org/teacher/ag_facts.cfm
Discover facts about the crops and livestock produced in each US state.

The United States: Her Natural & Industrial Resources
www.esri.com/products/maps-we-love/natural-resources
Explore the many natural resources in the United States using this interactive map.

INDEX